W9-CHO-883

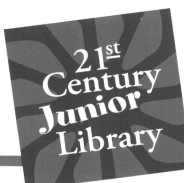

21st Century Junior Library

Coelophysis

by Josh Gregory

CHERRY LAKE PUBLISHING * ANN ARBOR, MICHIGAN

Published in the United States of America by Cherry Lake Publishing
Ann Arbor, Michigan
www.cherrylakepublishing.com

Content Adviser: Gregory M. Erickson, PhD, Paleontologist, Department of Biological Science,
Florida State University, Tallahassee, Florida

Reading Adviser: Marla Conn, Read With Me Now

Photo Credits: Cover and pages 10 and 16, © Michael Rosskothen/Shutterstock.com; pages 4
and 12, © Andreas Meyer/Shutterstock.com; pages 6, 14, and 18, © Kostyantyn Ivanyshen/
Shutterstock.com; page 8, Park Ranger / tinyurl.com/nztyug5 / CC-BY-2.0; page 20, Captmondo /
tinyurl.com/llwxnz7 / CC-BY-SA-3.0.

LIBRARY OF CONGRESS CATALOGING-IN-PUBLICATION DATA

Gregory, Josh, author.
  Coelophysis / by Josh Gregory.
    pages cm.—(Dinosaurs) (21st Century junior library)
  Summary: "Learn about the dinosaur known as Coelophysis, from what it ate to how it lived."—
Provided by publisher.
  Audience: K to grade 3.
  Includes bibliographical references and index.
  ISBN 978-1-63362-382-8 (lib. bdg.)—ISBN 978-1-63362-410-8 (pbk.)—
ISBN 978-1-63362-438-2 (pdf)—ISBN 978-1-63362-466-5 (e-book)
  1. Coelophysis—Juvenile literature. 2. Dinosaurs—Juvenile literature. I. Title.
QE862.S3G7668 2015
567.912–dc23   2014045655

Cherry Lake Publishing would like to acknowledge the work of
The Partnership for 21st Century Skills.
Please visit www.p21.org for more information.

Printed in the United States of America
Corporate Graphics
July 2015

CONTENTS

Coelophysis was a dangerous hunter.

What Was Coelophysis?

A group of small dinosaurs moves quietly through the forest. They keep a close watch over the area. Suddenly, one of them darts forward. It has spotted a lizard among the plants ahead. The *Coelophysis* moves quickly. It snatches its **prey** in its jaws. Time to eat!

Coelophysis thrived hundreds of millions of years ago.

Coelophysis once lived in what is now the southwestern United States. It lived about 203 million to 196 million years ago. This means it was one of the first dinosaurs on Earth. But like all dinosaurs, *Coelophysis* is now **extinct**.

Ask Questions! Have you ever been to the southwestern United States? What is it like? What do you think it was like when *Coelophysis* lived? If you don't know, ask! A librarian or teacher can help you find out what you want to know.

Experts are not sure what colors *Coelophysis* might have been.

What Did *Coelophysis* Look Like?

Coelophysis was smaller than most other dinosaurs. It was only about 9.8 feet (3 meters) long. It weighed about 40 to 50 pounds (18 to 23 kilograms). This means it was about as heavy as a large dog.

Coelophysis never walked on its short front legs.

Coelophysis stood on its strong back legs. Its long tail helped it stay balanced. It used its small front legs to grab food. Each of *Coelophysis*'s four legs had three toes. The toes ended in sharp claws.

Look!

Take a close look at a picture of *Coelophysis*. Does it look like any other dinosaurs you have seen? What about other kinds of animals? How do you think *Coelophysis* looked while it was moving?

Coelophysis's long neck was very flexible.

Coelophysis had a long neck. Its head was long and thin. Its mouth opened like a crocodile's. Inside the mouth were many teeth. They were very sharp. They also had jagged edges. This made them perfect for cutting through meat.

Coelophysis could easily outrun many
other animals.

How Did *Coelophysis* Live?

The name *Coelophysis* means "**hollow** form." This name comes from the dinosaur's hollow bones. Being hollow made the bones lightweight. This helped make *Coelophysis* fast and **agile**. These skills were important to *Coelophysis*. They helped it survive in a dangerous world.

Coelophysis might have used its nose to help sniff out nearby prey or predators.

Coelophysis used its speed to catch prey. It hunted other small dinosaurs. It also ate lizards and small crocodiles. Such small prey was probably swallowed whole.

Coelophysis also used its speed to flee dangerous **predators**. These predators included larger dinosaurs. When attacked, *Coelophysis* could hop out of the way. Then it ran to safety.

Coelophysis groups worked together to find food.

Coelophysis probably lived in groups called herds. Most animals that live in herds are plant eaters. But *Coelophysis* was a hunter.

Staying in a herd would have helped keep *Coelophysis* safe. Herd members could look out for each other. They also hunted together like wolves do today. They probably even shared food.

This *Coelophysis* skeleton can be seen at the
Redpath Museum in Montreal, Quebec, in Canada.

We learn about *Coelophysis* by studying its **fossils**. The first *Coelophysis* fossils were found in New Mexico. Others were found in Arizona. Scientists have even discovered whole *Coelophysis* **skeletons**! This helped them learn about the dinosaur's size and shape. Some fossils even include what the *Coelophysis* had last eaten!

Make a Guess!

People have discovered huge groups of *Coelophysis* fossils together. Many skeletons were right on top of each other. What does this tell us about the way *Coelophysis* lived? Search online or visit a library to find the answer. Did you guess correctly?

GLOSSARY

agile (AJ-il) able to move and dart about quickly

extinct (ek-STINGKT) describing a type of plant or animal that has completely died out

fossils (FAH-suhlz) the preserved remains of living things from thousands or millions of years ago

hollow (HAH-loh) empty on the inside

predators (PRED-uh-turz) animals that live by hunting other animals for food

prey (PRAY) an animal that is hunted by other animals for food

skeletons (SKEL-uh-tuhnz) the frameworks of bones that support and protect the bodies of animals

FIND OUT MORE

BOOKS

Dixon, Dougal. *Coelophysis and Other Dinosaurs of the South*. Minneapolis: Picture Window Books, 2007.

Gray, Susan Heinrichs. *Coelophysis*. Chanhassen, MN: The Child's World, 2004.

WEB SITES

Coelophysis—New Mexico's State Fossil

http://nmstatefossil.org
Find out why *Coelophysis* was chosen as the official state fossil of New Mexico.

HowStuffWorks—Coelophysis

http://animals.howstuffworks.com /dinosaurs/coelophysis.htm
Learn more about how *Coelophysis* lived.

INDEX

ABOUT THE AUTHOR

Josh Gregory writes and edits books for kids. He lives in Chicago, Illinois.